DIVINE DREAMS

OF THE
END TIMES

The Work of the Holy Spirit in the Last Days

Isabel Nodoli Radebe

THE JESUS IS COMING MINISTRY BORN FROM DEVINE DREAMS ABOUT THE END TIMES

LCCN: 2026904288

ISBN
978-1-964035-36-9 (Paperback)
978-1-964035-35-2 (eBook)

JOEL 2:28

ACTS 2:17

"And it shall come to pass afterward. That I will pour out My Spirit on all flesh; Your sons and your daughters shall prophesy, Your old men shall dream dreams, Your young men shall see visions."

TABLE OF CONTENTS

ABOUT THE AUTHOR

Isabel Nodoli Radebe was born in the village of Bizana in the Eastern Cape of South Africa, though she was raised in Gauteng in the township of Evaton. Like many others, she and her siblings were raised by their mother after a divorce between their mother and father. At the age of 19, she was raped by a prominent member of society, and in those days, her mother did not have the resources to take her for counselling. Through the prayer of her mother and siblings, the HOLY SPIRIT healed the wounds of her broken heart as written in Psalm 147:3, where the bible says, "He heals the brokenhearted and binds up their wounds". Her mother went through many things which caused her chronic illness to intensify until her death in 2008. She also lost a sister and two brothers, and thanks GOD to this day that her other siblings are still alive.

Before South Africa was liberated, she went to exile with other youth and came back home just before 1994. She then had a son whose father died in exile after contracting malaria, and after eight years she got married. After five years of marriage, in 2004, her husband passed away of pneumonia.

In 2006, she left politics and since then has been doing GOD's work. She relocated to New Zealand in April, 2006, to work there as a Civil Engineer until December 2010. The relocation happened after she completed Bible School, and GOD used her in 2009 at Elim Church in Papatoetoe Auckland under Pastor Rattan Sigh for a specific purpose, where she assisted the Senior Pastor. She had Devine Dreams whilst she was working in New Zealand which are in this book and they were all about the End Times and Rapture of the Church (the Coming of JESUS).

Coming back home to South Africa, she became focused on pastoring at Vaal Sons and Daughters Aglow Fellowship Ministry under Bishop Lindiwe Mkhonza who lives in Pretoria and Apostle Motsepe who lives in the Vaal. Since from March 2015 the ministry extended from Sons and Daughters Aglow Fellowship to JESUS is Coming Ministry reaching out to nations. She is also evangelizing under "Ear2Hear Global Ministry". After moving to Pretoria, she is currently attending the Gospel Teachings at Living Word in Pretoria East as a home church.

INTRODUCTION

The purpose of this book is tell the world about the Devine Dreams messages about the End Times as this was a promise from GOD as written in Joel 2:28 and Apostle Peter received this promise in the book of Acts 2:17. 1:14; 21:9. We are living in the times of the Outpouring of the HOLY SPIRIT. The promise was emphasizing on "old men dreaming dreams", since the Spirit is poured out to all flesh women are not excluded from spiritual gifts and powers and this is written in the book of Acts 1:14

> *"These all continued with one accord in prayer and supplication, with the women and Mary the mother of Jesus, and with His brothers."*

In the book of Acts 1:14

> *"Now this man had four virgin daughters who prophesied."*

A divine dream is a glimpse of what God has a person's future or for the nation/s which and since it is the promise of GOD which is biblically, it will be in line with the Word of God (leading to a certain scripture of future prophetic message that need to come to pass). The emphasis is to remind people about what will come to pass in the near future.

In the Devine dream many times, one will be the main character and others will also be there as well depending on the message conveyed. The Devine Dream takes you to the future vision and glimpse of activities happening at a person's spiritual sight and one is actively a participant in what is happening at that moment until that scene is complete. When the scene is complete, the person may wake up. I normally write down what I saw in the dream and relate it to the biblical scriptures since I know following that will be the manifestation of it physically in future.

Devine dreams must be aligned to the Word of GOD because they are live messages that come from GOD to remind people about what is about to come since GOD does communicate with us through dreams. I have learned that no matter the message is, if the HOLY SPIRIT allows me to share it, I must obey GOD and do as instruct and we read about Joseph's obedience in Genesis 37:1-44:9, he told them inspite of their unbelief. It is good to obey GOD than to fear men as it is written in Proverbs 9:10:-

> *"The fear of the Lord is the beginning of wisdom, And*
> *the knowledge of the Holy One is understanding."*

This book reveal the Work of the HOLY SPIRIT and HIS attributes as:-

HE is Sovereign – To show His Sovereignty, in Genesis 1:2 we read that the earth was without form, and void; and darkness was on the face of the deep. The Spirit of God was hovering over the face of the waters. The Holy Spirit was there in the creation to put the earth in order because He Himself sets the standard as there is no standard or criterion higher than that set by Him to judge upon, because He is Sovereign even over the creation. We need to acknowledge His deity (1 Corinthians 12:3) and submit to His authority so we can rest in His care because He is the Almighty One whose power manifested even in the creation of the Universe.

HE is Omnipresence – In Psalm 139:7 David confirms the omnipresence of the Holy Spirit when he said; he cannot hide from the presence of the Holy Spirit because He is present everywhere at the same time and eternally. He was there in the creation and He could not be trapped in the creation because He is transcendent, and at the same time He is close to us and also dwells in us (John 14:17 and 1 Corinthians 3:16). His ministry today is universal at the same time.

HE is Omnipotent – Having unlimited power as written in Acts 1:8, Jesus spoke about the power of the Holy Spirit because without His incomparable greatest power, witnessing will be powerless. The power of the Holy Spirit is demonstrated in Luke 4:14 where it confirms that Jesus went out preaching in the power of the Holy Spirit and Jesus' words was with power and authority. We cannot ignore His Omnipotent Power because, even witnessing without Him is powerless which is like labouring in vain. He also has power to control our lives once we allow Him so He can lead us to do God's will over ours. His power is the power that also raised Jesus from the dead (Romans 8:11), and this power is available to us to witness for Christ and to live a victorious life over evil.

HE is Omniscience – He knows everything that happened yesterday, and that is happening today, and that is to happen tomorrow because He is the Omnipresent and the Omnipotent. He is the only One who reveals mysterious things as He was there in the creation of heavens and the earth. In 1 Corinthians 2:11, it is written that no one who knows the things of God except the Spirit of God who reveals them to those who believe in the Lord Jesus (John 16:13).

HE is a Faithfull GOD – In the midst of the End Times turbulences of life we know that HIS Character is the same forever. Our lives are in HIS safe HANDS because of HIS Faithfulness. Prophet Jeremiah expressed the belief in GOD's restoration after the destruction of Jerusalem by the Babylonians that the same Faithfull GOD said HE will also restore the City and that was all Jeremiah needed. Even today in the midst of turmols we believe in HIM because HE is Faithful, Sovereign, Omnipresence, Omnipotence and Omniscience.

In closing, the Devine Dreams is all about the Work of the HOLY SPIRIT today the End Times (for the Work of the HOLY SPIRIT refer to this Title published is 2013 which is all about HIM being our comforter, being an advocate on our behalf, counselling, leading, teaching, instructing, judging, conviction and converting, guide us into all truth.

PREFACE

The Rapture and the Second Coming of Christ

[16]"For the Lord Himself will descend from heaven with a shout, with the voice of an archangel, and with the trumpet of GOD. And the dead in Christ will rise first. [17]Then we who are alive and remain shall be caught up together with them in the clouds to meet the Lord in the air. And thus, we shall always be with the Lord."

- 1 Thessalonians 4:16-17

"Watch therefore, and pray always that you may be counted worthy to escape all these things that will come to pass, and to stand before the Son of Man."

- Luke 21:36

While we were still sinners, Christ died for us. The scripture says, and I quote,

"⁹ that if you confess with your mouth the Lord Jesus and believe in
your heart that GOD has raised Him from the dead, you will be
saved. ¹⁰ For with the heart one believes unto righteousness, and with
the mouth confession is made unto salvation. ¹¹For the Scripture
says, 'Whoever believes on Him will not be put to shame.' ¹² For there
is no distinction between Jew and Greek, for the same Lord over
all is rich to all who call upon Him. ¹³ For 'whoever calls on
the name of the LORD *shall be saved'."* **- Romans 10:9-13**

The Messiah (JESUS CHRIST of Nazareth) was born into this world because Adam and Eve failed to carry out GOD's mandate to glorify Him in their lives. It was left for the Son of GOD, thousands of years later, to ultimately fulfill the divine revelation of GOD's character and purpose for man. JESUS had to be born to remove the sins of humankind through a perfect sacrifice of HIS own blood which HE shed for us on the cross. HIS purpose was to save and spread the Gospel of Salvation, the Good News, to individuals, and of the Kingdom to all nations.

Please note that reading this book does not replace your reading of the Bible. You are encouraged to read your Holy Bible more than any other book as the HOLY SPIRIT will give you the revelation as you read HIS Word.

In this book, I will choose not to interpret these dreams and visions since I am not gifted in that area. Therefore, I will simply present a dream, and the reader should pray and ask GOD for its interpretation. It is only GOD the HOLY SPIRIT who give gifts to us. As it is written in the book of 1 Corinthians 12, I am just a vessel to do HIS work. I humble myself as I write these dreams. I am nobody without the HOLY SPIRIT and I know nothing without HIM. In 2 Corinthians 12:1-6, Paul says the following words:

1"It is doubtless not profitable for me to boast. I will come to visions and revelations of the Lord: 2I know a man in Christ who fourteen years ago whether in the body I do not know, or whether out of the body I do not know, GOD knows such a one was caught up to the third heaven. 3And I know such a man whether in the body or out of the body I do not know, GOD knows 4how he was caught up into Paradise and heard inexpressible words, which it is not lawful for a man to utter. 5Of such a one I will boast; yet of myself I will not boast, except in my infirmities. 6For though I might desire to boast, I will not be a fool; for I will speak the truth. But I refrain, lest anyone should think of me above what he sees me to be or hears from me."

As I have said earlier, it was not in my plan to write this book, but I am following the lead of the HOLY SPIRIT by faith. I believe GOD is allowing me to write about the dreams of being in heaven because HE wants you to know that the message below is not from me but sent by HIM. I am nobody without the presence of the HOLY SPIRIT and I know nothing without HIM alone.

THE DEVINE
DREAMS

DREAM #1:
THE OLD TESTAMENT PROPHETS

I had this dream during my work in New Zealand (NZL) during 2008. I saw myself in heaven, but I did not see how I reached it. I saw myself walking with the LORD. HE was holding me by my right hand and when I looked at myself, I was a little schoolboy wearing a school uniform even though there were no changes in my inner spirit man, I was still me. As the book of Romans 8:9 says,

"But you are not in the flesh but in the Spirit, if indeed the Spirit of GOD dwells in you. Now if anyone does not have the Spirit of Christ, he is not His."

JESUS and I were walking in a field of beautiful blossoming yellow sunflowers of the height of about half a meter. These were all over the field and the LORD said HE would show me Father Abraham and other Old Testament Prophets. We walked a long distance, and I was bouncing with joy as I walked, but we walked until I was exhausted without seeing the end of the sunflowers, and I woke up before we reached the Old Testament Prophets.

According to www.wholeblossoms.com, sunflowers symbolize deep love. A person who has loved with sincerity and purity never forgets. On the contrary, this person absolutely loves until the end. The flower that most expresses fidelity is the sunflower. The sunflower is the symbol of the sun and symbolizes love and admiration.

DREAM #2:
THE LORD SUPPLYING DURING DROUGHT

It was in 2008 whilst I was still working in Taupo, New Zealand, and in my dream I was in the remotest land that I had never seen before. It was like I was on another planet. There was severe drought and hunger in that land. The soil was red and very dry and there was only a small portion of grass, like faded winter grass, even though it was summertime – it was an extremely hot sunny day. I did not see any houses there except an old church building, small but high in stature. People were queuing for food. The queue was not a straight queue; it was winding and exceptionally long. These people were all old, pale, and extremely hungry. Next to this old church structure (a simple mud structure), which was empty, there was a small, old table, and I went to the table. On top of the table, there were a few bundles of spinach and cabbage. The table was next to a small tree which could not even cover the table with shade.

The LORD was there, standing next to the table, looking at HIS people. HE then told me to feed these people in the queue; there were two other people who were also helping at the table. I looked at this meagre supply of food and I thought inside of my heart, the supply will not be enough to feed such a long queue of people, but I did not say it verbally. But, in my mind, I realized that the LORD can multiply the supply of food, so I did as commanded. I then started to distribute these vegetables to these old people. I realized the queue was moving and the food supply was always available on the table. These people were not pushing one another, they were so obedient, following the queue with dignity. As I distributed further, I understood that the LORD was supplying our needs and I must not worry about any supply shortages. HE stood there watching. I woke up still serving them. That was the end of the dream.

DREAM #3:
SEEING JESUS WITH WOUNDS IN HIS FEET

I was still in New Zealand in 2009, working in Auckland and assisting the Senior Pastor at a church in Papatoetoe. During this time, I was spending a lot of time in prayer as a result of having few friends from the church and at home. My Greatest Friend was the LORD HIMSELF. One day, on a Saturday, I prayed for about six hours in my dining room. During the prayer, I distinctly felt the pain of losing my mother and my husband. I also remembered my friend in South Africa who I could not reach even by telephone. I started to cry to the LORD loudly, saying,

"LORD, I have lost my mom and my husband, the worst part is my friend is in SA. I feel lonely, I need someone just to hug me."

Remember, I quoted Romans 8:9 above which says,

"But you are not in the flesh but in the Spirit, if indeed the Spirit of GOD dwells in you. Now if anyone does not have the Spirit of Christ, he is not His."

As I was crying, the HOLY SPIRIT came, and I saw my spirit body coming out of my physical body. We flew together past the second heaven to the third heaven. There in the clouds (I believe this is the second heaven), there was such heaviness, but once we passed through, there was such a refreshing air, I still remember it vividly. Then I saw a wide river full of water and we had to cross it to the other side. Because the HOLY SPIRIT is SOVEREIGN, we crossed over it without touching the waters. When we landed on the other side of the river, my eyes were facing down, and I saw His feet with the open holes of wounds (Luke 24:40; John 20:20). I immediately realized that this was the LORD JESUS CHRIST who was crucified for our sins on the cross of Calvary.

People may ask how I knew that I was with the HOLY SPIRIT. I knew in my spirit and I could feel HIS presence behind me on my right-hand side, though I did not turn to look at HIM. Then I stood up. The LORD did not say anything, but HE walked away from us towards a half egg-shaped tunnel and we followed HIM, walking on the ground now. It was not a long distance from where we were. At the entrance of this tunnel, I started repeating the same words I said when I was praying in my house,

"LORD, I have lost my mom and my husband, the worst part is my friend is in SA. I feel lonely, I need someone just to hug me."

Without saying a word in response, HE stretched HIS HAND to touch me. Immediately after HIS touch, I saw my body shrinking and I became a baby wearing a diaper, but, in my spirit, my inner man, I was still the same person who could think and reason as an adult. HE took me and cradled me in HIS arms. HE held me only for very few minutes and in HIS HANDS, I felt the LOVE of GOD, and I was saying in my heart, "Please do not put me down." Right now, when I think about that LOVE of GOD that I felt in HIS HANDS, tears begin to fill my eyes because I really wanted to be with HIM. HE did not hold me for as long a time as I wished, and HE then put me down without saying a word. When HE put me down, my body size went back to its normal height and HE turned and took three steps, entering the tunnel. I realized that HE was leaving me, and I couldn't just be quiet otherwise I wouldn't see HIM again. I said to HIM,

"LORD, please, I want to come."

Then HE responded for the first time. HE said,

"NO, THERE IS STILL A LOT TO BE DONE."

I am quoting HIS Words as they are in John 14:15-18,

Jesus Promises another Helper

"If you love Me, [b]keep My commandments. 16And I will pray the Father, and He will give you another [c]Helper, that He may abide with you forever— 17the Spirit of truth, whom the world cannot receive, because it neither sees Him nor knows Him; but you know Him, for

He dwells with you and will be in you. 18I will not leave you orphans; I will come to you."

After saying that, HE turned and went into the tunnel, and the HOLY SPIRIT immediately took me back to earth and I entered my physical body in the dining room where I was praying.

The message I got from this dream is that, through prayer, I was asking GOD to send someone physically just to give me a hug because I felt lonely; the Bible says there is nothing impossible for GOD.

"For with GOD nothing will be impossible." - Luke 1:37

Instead, HE HIMSELF hugged me. When we pray, we must know that HE hears our prayers as is said in the book of 1 John 5:14,

"This is the confidence we have in approaching GOD: that if we ask anything according to his will, he hears us."

HE is ever compassionate with our daily travails of life, though HE said there is still more work to be done. HE did not explain where, but we all know the Great Commission of Matthew 28:18-20 where HE told us to spread the Gospel of Salvation to the Ends of the Earth and HE will be with us. The important thing to say is that I was praying a simple prayer using my own words, GOD heard my prayer. Let us note that, HE answers prayers in HIS own timing, not our timing. And HIS timing is perfect. Sometimes we prayed and HE delays to answer for a reason, we therefore need to be persistent in our request as said in the book of 1 Thessalonian 5:17 where we are told to pray without ceasing or constantly.

DREAM #4: JESUS PURIFYING MY HEART

It was in April, 2010, and I was still working in New Zealand but attending church services in a Wellington Lower Hutt Church. We were waiting for the yearly "Fire Conference" and one day as I was leaving for church, I touched my door and immediately started to have unbearable back pain to the extent that I could not walk properly. It was not the first time I had experienced back pain but this was unbearable. I had to stay at home during that week and did not go to work from Monday to Friday. What could I do in a foreign land alone during the day and night except to pray? I was praying day and night on each day.

On Thursday of that week as I was kneeling down praying only in spirit that time, the HOLY SPIRIT came, and my spirit inner man was taken out of my physical body again. We went to the third heaven, passing the so-called second heaven as I said before. After crossing a wide river, we landed at a glass sliding door. Again, I could feel the presence of the HOLY SPIRIT on my right side slightly behind me and I did not turn to look at HIM. I knelt down at the door and continued to pray in spirit as I did in my house, and the sliding door was opened. We entered and the HOLY SPIRIT was my HELPER (John 14:26). I knelt down again just near the sliding door and inside the open office-like space. I saw the LORD at the far end of the biggest round table, sitting with HIS elders who surrounded HIM. HE was facing my direction. I kept on praying in spirit and HE did not say anything except to point HIS Right Finger to my heart, and I immediately felt a sharp pain in my heart. It came to my inner man that the LORD JESUS was purifying my heart. After that, I saw my spirit body entering my physical body in the same room I had been praying in without noticing how I left heaven to come back to earth.

The lesson that I learned through this dream is that GOD does listen to ordinary prayer if we pray earnestly, and HE also listens to the ones who are praying in spirit in the same manner. There is no prayer that is not important to HIM. But we must remember the Apostle Paul in Jude 20-21 where he is encouraging us to always pray in Spirit, so we maintain our lives with GOD.

"20But you, beloved, building yourselves up on your most holy faith, praying in the Holy Spirit, 21keep yourselves in the love of GOD, (c) looking for the mercy of our Lord Jesus Christ unto eternal life."

DREAM #5: HEARING A VOICE FROM HEAVEN

It was in 2010 when I had this dream. Though I was still living in New Zealand in reality, in the dream I was living in my mama's house in Evaton, South Africa, and I was thirsty for attending the church service at Sebokeng, Zone 14. I had to wait for six days to attend the church service. The day of the service came and, on that day, the sun was shining so clear; beautiful in its status without even a single cloud in the sky. At the center of this location, there was a church by the name of El-Shaddai (big in its structure). It was my first time attending this church and I was in a hurry, thinking the service had already started and I was late. When I entered El-Shaddai, sweating due to running, I found that there was no church service but there were students wearing school uniforms (black and white uniforms). They were singing, preparing for school choir competitions right at the time of church service *(refer to the book of Revelation 2 and 3, where the LORD JESUS is rebuking and commending Churches of the End Times according to their works*

– any RED notes in the Bible refer to Words from JESUS HIMSELF and people ignore them even though they call themselves "the followers of JESUS", so painful is that). So, disappointed, I then left and tried to find another church service nearby. When I found one, I entered, and inside the church, people were wearing traditional clothes also preparing for traditional competitions.

I looked at the time and realized that I would be too late to search for another church service even though I was very thirsty for the Word of the LORD. But I did not lose hope, I went to a few more churches without any success in finding a church preaching the Word of GOD. In all these churches that I visited, they were focused on their earthly issues instead of the Word of GOD.

Because I was running from church to church, I became tired on that clear, very sunny day, and, looking for a resting place, I saw a big rock in an open field where a boy sat. I went to this rock and joined him just to relax a little bit under that extreme sunshine. I did not have any umbrella or see any tree to sit under. We did not say a word to one another. I only wiped my sweat with my hand, then I decided to return home to wait for the next Sunday church service after the disappointment of not finding one on that day. As I walked, I heard a loud voice coming from the sky saying,

"You are not alone; you are with MY HOLY SPIRIT."

The echoing voice was so loud, but it was only me who heard the message since people were busy doing their own things. I clearly understood that this was the voice of the LORD JESUS. After the shock of this echoing voice, I woke up. Even though I do not have the gift of interpreting dreams, I believe this is related to the churches of Revelation 2 and 3 where the Church of Laodicea is called to repent

Paul in 1 Corinthians 6:12 says,

"All things are lawful for me, but all things are not helpful. All things are lawful for me, but I will not be brought under the power of any."

Note that everything in today's world is allowable and others are correct according to government laws, but those things may not be correct based on biblical living principles. Some actions may hurt others, anything we do that hurts rather than helps to build others is not right. Again, there are things that are not sinful in themselves, but they are not good because they can dominate and lead us away from God. Freedom is a mark of the Christian faith but we need not to abuse it allowing our actions to grow into bad habits that would control and lead us away from God. Jesus warned the Church of Laodicea about this kind of freedom leading this Church to focus on self-satisfaction pleasures rather than drawing near to Him as it is written in Revelations 3:19 which says,

"As many as I love, I rebuke and chasten. Therefore be zealous and repent.

The call here is to allow the Holy Spirit to re-ignite our zeal for God because in most cases, freedom and the pleasures of this world (money, security and material possessions and so forth) could sometimes be dangerous, and their temporary satisfaction could make us indifferent to God's offer of lasting satisfaction. Sometimes if we allow these things to dominate our minds, slowly we begin to shut God out of our lives until we idolize these possessions. Just as the spark of love can be rekindled in any relationship, so the Holy Spirit can re-ignite our zeal back to God once again. To repent from being away from God due to world possession, Jesus said this Church, could still buy the real gold from Him or real spiritual treasures that are available in Him.

It was discovered that the Laodicea's were situated in a place that was famous for its beauty, wealth and its city was also a centre for banking and other financial operations. Laodicea was the home of one of the seven churches addressed in the book of Revelation and that Church is/ was apparently taken with the atmosphere of focusing in material things which led them to be lukewarm in their spirit lives. Jesus is also advising us today to buy from Him gold refined in the fire instead, so we could be rich because we may think that having luxury life is all that we live for which lead to self-centredness.

According to verse 17 and 18, this church claimed to be rich, wealthy, having no need to surrender to God because of great pride in financial wealth due to business activities, leading them away from spiritual desires. Most of us even today, we are so focus on world luxuries which is misleading because Jesus says this church claim to be rich whilst it is poor. As believers, God want His word to be in our spirit for eternity more than anything else. It is good to have material possession but these earthly things need not to be idolized because the love of them, lead to spiritual darkness where we end up forgetting to put our hearts on Christ as our Savoir, hence Jesus says we need to repent and be zealous once again.

We need to learn from what Jesus said to the Smyrna church (Revelation 2:9). He said He knew about their sufferings and poverty but commended them, that they are in fact rich, and He encouraged them to be faithful even when faced with death so they would receive the crown of life due to them being true witnesses in spite of hardships as opposed to His comments for the Laodicea's whose focus was on wealth rather than the spirit things. Jesus is encouraging us to have faith even during sufferings as a key point and not to lose focus.

In conclusion, in this End of the Age time, Jesus through His Holy Spirit is here, calling us to be zealous and repent from sin of neglecting our first love to Him. God is love by His nature and He cares for us, He doesn't want any soul to perish due to focus on world standard of living, hence He has sent the Holy Spirit to convict us once more, and there is no truth other than that. In spite of the fact that Christ is exalted above all, because of His compassion, He is standing at each door of our hearts, knocking to seek, save and finally to give us a gift of His Holy Spirit to lead and guide us during this hour so we can be zealous for good works.

The problem pointed out in the church of Laodicea's was to be lukewarm (neither hot nor cold – as written) which is happening today though we live in the last Days of Pentecost – the days where the Holy Spirit is here to help us, we need to allow Him once again to re-ignite that zeal so we can also serve Him during these end time. This zeal will able us to do what we are called to do during this Church dispensation.

DREAM #6:
THE ANGEL'S VISIT

In 2010, in another dream, I was sleeping on a single bed and a big man appeared. I understood he was an angel and I was not afraid. Once again, I saw my spirit body coming out of my physical body. The angel took me to the so-called second heaven, where my spirit felt heavy-laden. I was wearing a very thick garment that was jelly-like and transparent, the thickness of about 15cm. We entered the sky which was dark and very heavy. I saw many fallen angels busy planning to attack the believers here on earth. When I looked down to the earth during the night, I saw prayers of saints represented by protruding lights just like Christmas fireworks. Some of these fireworks died at lower levels, some persisted to higher levels, and only a few penetrated the second heaven whilst very few passed through to the third heaven. These represented prayer warriors who were praying to destroy the plans of the enemy because there is power in prayer. There are times when we become weary even to pray earnestly, and we pray amiss. I was reading the book of James 4:3-4 and it says the following:

> "³You ask and do not receive, because you ask amiss,
> that you may spend it on your pleasures. ⁴Adulterers and
> adulteresses! Do you not know that friendship with the
> world is enmity with GOD? Whoever therefore wants to be
> a friend of the world makes himself an enemy of GOD."

Because of the garment that I was wearing and being with the big angel – a giant compared to normal men – I managed to see the fallen world, but they could not see me.

———

I am writing these things through the Work of the HOLY SPIRIT. Remember, GOD is above all authorities, Satan had to ask GOD to test Job. He cannot do anything if GOD, who is the CREATOR, does not allow him. The HOLY SPIRIT is in me, all these dreams are revealed to show the GLORY of our LIVING GOD in JESUS NAME. Again, GOD is revealing these dreams, so you know that I am sent by HIM to tell you about the Coming of CHRIST very soon. In Zechariah 4:6, the LORD said to Zerubbabel,

> "This is the word of the Lord to Zerubbabel:
> 'Not by might nor by power, but by My Spirit,'
> Says the Lord of hosts."

The name Zerubbabel biblically means: A stranger at Babylon, dispersion of confusion.

The LORD took me from South Africa to New Zealand to teach me HIS ways. I know this because I had most of the dreams in New Zealand where I did not have many friends. HE was my best friend. Coming back to South Africa these dreams stopped, and besides those I had before leaving South Africa, I did not have another one except to start writing the first book. I relate all these dreams to you in JESUS NAME through the Work of the HOLY SPIRIT. Amen.

DREAM #7: COSMIC DISTURBANCES AND PURIFICATION

GOD said in Joel 2:28-29,

28"And it shall come to pass afterward that I will pour out My Spirit on all flesh; Your sons and your daughters shall prophesy, your old men shall dream dreams, your young men shall see visions. 29And also on My menservants and on My maidservants, I will pour out My Spirit in those days."

I thank GOD for revealing things of the Spirit through dreams and visions to me as a vessel because the outpouring of the HOLY SPIRIT has already come. The Apostle Peter, being full of the power of the Holy Ghost in Acts 2:17-18 quoted Joel's prophesies as being fulfilled because GOD is faithful, and this outpouring will continue even after the church is caught up or raptured.

Below I will share with you a dream that came from GOD, it is in relation to the sealing of HIS chosen ones as written in Revelation 7. I must emphasize that the dream itself is not important, but referring to the word of GOD is important. As I said earlier, these dreams are there just as a small direction arrow pointing to GOD's Word.

The Dream

Extremely Distressing Cosmic Conditions

It was on Saturday, 9 April, 2005, when I fell into a deep sleep and began to dream. In this dream, I was in my grandmother's house in the township of Evaton, situated in the southern part of Johannesburg in South Africa. I dreamed of an extraordinary darkened and sorrowful world condition, and I saw nothing (not even people, birds, cars, etc.) moving outside, although it was daytime. All were inside their houses as if there was an extreme distress and mourning. People were grieved by something, and I was shocked by these worldwide conditions where there was no work, school in fact no movement at the streets though I did not know the course of this grieving and mourning. This outside condition also made me sit inside my granny's house.

The Lord appeared

As I was sitting in the house, the LORD appeared in human form with four other ordinary men, entering the house through the front door. HE was tall with long, shiny hair, wearing a long robe, and I understood in the dream that the man wearing the robe was the LORD. Without saying anything, HE took a candle and its candlestick which were on top of a very old-fashioned table in the kitchen and lit the candle to give light, and there was light inside the house (Exodus 10:22-23).

HE then went outside and we all followed HIM towards my mother's house which was about 200m from my granny's house. Along the way, as we followed HIM, the LORD began to preach on just one subject. I quote HIS Words,

"REPENT, THE KINGDOM OF HEAVEN IS NEAR."

HE repeated this message again and again until we reached my mother's house.

Watchfulness required for HIS Coming

My mother's house had two external doors facing the same direction and an internal door adjoining the two rooms, and the LORD entered the house with two men, using the second entrance, and I also entered the house with the other two men, using the first door. The door that we used led us to a group of men; half of them were just standing as if they were waiting for something, and the other half were in a very deep sleep on the floor. I went to the men who were sleeping and tried to wake them up so we could all go and listen to the LORD's message, but all I said to them was in vain because they would not wake up. Eventually, I gave up and left them.

I then spoke to those who were standing, explaining that the LORD wanted us to be ready because HE says the kingdom of heaven is near, and these men were able to listen directly to the LORD's voice because they were alert.

Purification process observed

As the dream continued, the LORD went outside with the same two men HE had entered with, and we also went outside, leaving the others as they were in the house (some standing and others still sleeping).

As we were outside, a young woman in her mid-thirties came running towards us. She was so excited, telling us that she was preparing for her marriage which was to take place soon, and after she finished talking, the LORD placed HIS right hand on top of the head of this young woman without saying anything, and water came out of HIS hand over this woman like water coming out of a shower.

All of us were amazed as we watched the water coming from HIS hand; the LORD did not say anything, but water kept on showering the woman. I saw this water penetrating the brain, going through the chest and inner parts of the body, which was suddenly transparent. I immediately understood in my spirit that this was a purification process that the woman was going through, and the woman was very obedient throughout this process. Then the water stopped, and the woman was obedient until the completion of this process.

The LORD ascends to heaven

After the water stopped, the LORD didn't say a word, but as we were looking, He ascended slowly, and we watched, raising our heads until

HE entered the sky, and we could not see HIM anymore due to clouds covering HIM. HE did not ascend quickly, but HE ascended slowly before our eyes until HE disappeared into the clouds of the sky. After HE entered the clouds, we then lowered our heads slowly until we were able to see one another.

Another woman who was about to give birth to a baby

Then the purified woman began to preach the same words that the LORD said, very powerful although the woman was not there when HE preached. Along the way as we follow this young woman, we met a pregnant woman who was waiting to give birth to a child. The woman began to have pre-birth pains. The purified woman asked her if she would like her to pray for her pre-birth pain and the pregnant one agreed. Being filled with the power of the HOLY SPIRIT, the purified women then laid her hands on the pregnant woman and prayed, "Be healed in JESUS' NAME". The pregnant woman confirmed that the pain was gone right there, and we then left her. We kept walking, listening to this purified woman whilst the world was still in the state of sorrowful and distressed conditions. As we were walking, my alarm clock rang, and I woke up to prepare for work. The message was all about repentance during these End Times.

DREAM #8: THE BOOK OF DANIEL 8 AND THE REVELATION

Daniel 8:1-14 tells us that, in a vision, Daniel saw himself at the fortress of Susa, in the province of Elam as he was standing beside the Ulai River. As he looked, he saw a ram with two long horns standing beside the river. One of the horns was longer than the other, even though it had grown later than the other one. The ram butted everything out of his way to the west, to the north, and to the south, and no one could stand against him or help his victims. He did as he pleased and became very great. Whilst he was watching, suddenly a he goat appeared from the west, crossing the land so swiftly that he didn't even touch the ground.

This goat, which had one very large horn between its eyes, headed toward the two-horn ram that he had seen standing beside the river, rushing at him in a rage. The goat charged furiously at the ram and struck him, breaking off both his horns. And the ram became helpless, the he goat continue to knock him down and trampled him. No one who was able to rescue the ram from the goat's power as the goat became very powerful. But at the height of his power, his large horn was broken off. In the large horn's place grew four prominent horns pointing in the four directions of the earth. Some of these prophecies were fulfilled and some still to come.

As we began before our brief history and future lesson, in the dream I saw myself in the center of the earth, which I now know is Turkey. Here, I saw myself watching a war between the he-goat and the ram at the Euphrates River which is found in the book of Revelation. I cannot tell how I reached that land, but I saw myself in that land where I had never been before, standing alone against a tree, hiding in shock of what I witnessed. The trees were lining the opposite side of the river to where I stood. On the other side of the river, I saw exactly what is in the above picture – the he-goat with a notable horn between his eyes and the ram with two horns lying beside the river. Both were huge, their bodies bigger than the houses which were a little distance from the river.

Near the houses and the city, there were others also looking at the he-goat and the ram in shock. None of us could help the helpless ram when the he-goat charged furiously and trampled and stamped him with anger using his sharp horn. All of us who were watching were very helpless to rescue the ram from the he-goat's power as is written in Daniel 8. As I watched, a man appeared on the scene. This man was tall enough to see over the roofs of the houses.

He stood next to the he-goat and ram, and immediately, the he-goat left the ram. To me it was like the he-goat could not stand the presence of this man. On the appearance of this man, I noticed the he-goat immediately left, but walking with pride. It was very arrogant with its notable horn, entering the houses and the city of that area. I woke up whilst the he-goat was still on its way to the houses and the city. I did not record this dream as I used to in my journal until months later when I received the revelation from the Holy Spirit that there was something missing in my first book. As I said, I take these dreams as small direction arrows pointing to what the word of GOD says as written in Daniel 8.

We read in Daniel 8:24 parallel to the Anti-Christ of Revelation 6:2 as well as Revelation 9 to explain the dream-vision of Daniel:

That the Anti-Christ will destroy nations from the power given to him by the evil one. We also see the arrogance and the defiance toward GOD HIMSELF. The continuation of Daniel 7 and 8 is explained below in chapter 8. This does not specifically interpret what happened in the past kingdoms, but this book is all about the future. The above must be read in line with Daniel 7-12; Revelation 9, 13:7, and 16-19; Ezekiel 38 and 39, the Gog/Magog Conflict; Zechariah 10-14, and Psalm 83.

In the above dream, I was in the land that was in the center of the earth as I understood it. After the dream, I searched for the country that is geographically in the center of the earth, and I found Turkey, meaning in the dream I was in Turkey, at the Euphrates River, based on the HOLY SPIRIT'S revelation of my dream.

Revelation 9:13-16 tells us that one third of mankind will be killed at this river during the 70th week of Daniel (the last week of mankind's rule before CHRIST takes over to rule for eternity (Daniel 2:44-45). The church won't be there at this time, the church will be raptured before this happens. In 2 Thessalonians 2:7, we are told that the church is the one who restrains the lawlessness. The lawlessness will be revealed completely when the church is taken away.

I then began by searching the center of the world and its inclusion in "End Time Prophecies". Below are summaries from the abovementioned newsletter.

I encourage you to read the December 15, 2017, "Watch Jerusalem" Newsletter By David Vejil and Herbert W. Armstrong concerning the History of Turkey and Esau as well as how Turkey fits in to the Biblical End Time Prophecy.

"The key to the Turkish identity and their origins lies in their name, Ottoman. This name appears in biblical prophecy. Remarkably, the nation with this name was prophesied to be near Israel, in control of a major gateway, and to be a great empire in control of the Promised

Land for a time. This name is Teman—grandson of Esau, who was grandson of the patriarch Abraham."

Below is Turkey, identified as a major prophesized gateway during the Great Tribulation of the End Times:

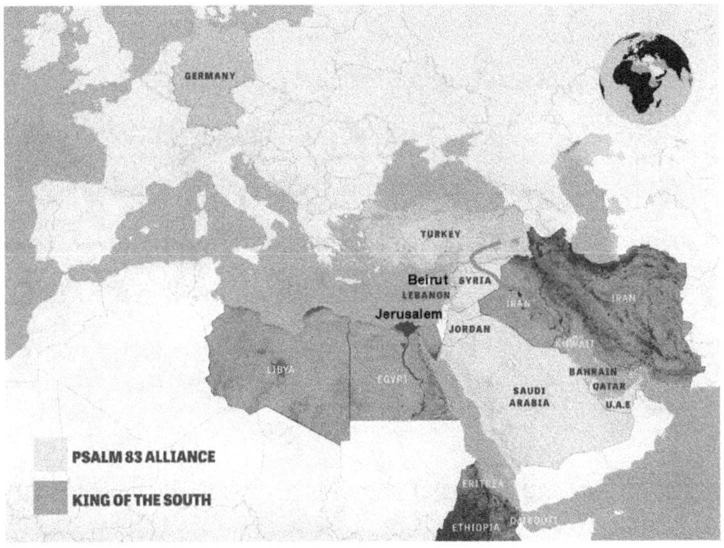

Source: Watch Jerusalem

Approx. Location of Euphrates River

The three main events scheduled under Revelation 9 to occur at the 2nd Woe (the 6th Trumpet), including Euphrates River Events (the Gulf River), are as follows:

1. **First Event:** *four mighty angels will be released from the Great River Euphrates. Leading a force of some 200,000,000 they will slay one third of mankind! (Rev. 9:13-15)*

2. **Second Event:** *the prophet is given a measuring rod and told to measure the Temple of GOD, the altar and them that worship therein. He is instructed not to measure the outer* court of the Temple, for it is given over to the Gentiles, who will be allowed to trample the holy city under foot for a period of 42 months. *(Rev. 11:1-2)*

3. **Third Event:** *during this same* 42 month period (1260 days) Yahweh's Two Witnesses will preach to the entire world. At the end of that time they will be murdered by the Beast who is to arise from out of the Abyss *(Rev. 11:3-7)* but after three-and-a-half days they will be raised to life and will ascend to heaven. The 2nd Woe (6th Trumpet) ends at the resurrection of the Two Witnesses *(Rev. 11:8-14)*.

We read in Daniel 8:20-22 that the interpretation of the Ram and He-Goat's location is as follows:

> *"20 The ram which you saw, having the two horns—they are the kings of **Media** and **Persia (The Old Ones)**. 21 And the male goat is the kingdom of **Greece (The Old Grecian Empire).** The large horn that is between its eyes is the first king. 22 As for the broken horn and the four that stood up in its place, four kingdoms shall arise out of that nation, but not with its power."*

The angel explained to Daniel in Daniel 7:7-8 the kingdoms that are destined to rule the world before Second Coming of CHRIST as follows:

"⁷After this I saw in the night visions, and behold, a fourth beast, dreadful and terrible, exceedingly strong. It had huge iron teeth; it was devouring, breaking in pieces, and trampling the residue with its feet. It was different from all the beasts that were before it, and it had ten horns. ⁸I was considering the horns, and there was another horn, a little one, coming up among them, before whom three of the first horns were plucked out by the roots. And there, in this horn, were eyes like the eyes of a man, and a mouth speaking pompous words."

The following graphic will help to demonstrate the kingdoms that Daniel saw troubling Israel before the Second Coming of Christ:

I was trying to establish the reason behind my dream where I saw myself at the center of the earth, Turkey, surrounded by Euphrates River, connecting it to the last kingdom mentioned in Daniel 2, 7 and 8 as summarized in the table below:

Daniel 2:32-34	Daniel 7:4-7	Daniel 8	
Head of Gold : Babylon Kingdom	Beast looked like a Lion with wings of an eagle	Not mentioned.	Past
Chest and Arms Silver: Media-Persia	Beast looked like a bear with three ribs in its mouth between its teeth	Ram with two horns symbolizing Media-Persia	
Belly and thighs Bronze: Greece	Beast looked like a leopard and on its back had four wings like those of a bird and four heads.	He-Goat horn and four horns raised under Grecian Empire (four divisions of Alexander the Great. History tells us that Alexander the Great overthrew the Turkish Empire before his death, then the four divisions took over.	
Legs of Iron: The Revival of the Great Ancient Rome Kingdom	Beast appears terrifying and frightening without description except for large iron teeth and ten horns.	Rome concurred the above four divisions and the little horn comes out from this kingdom. These Kingdoms of Alexandre the Great were: the Ptolemaic Kingdom of Egypt, the Seleucid Empire, the Attalid Dynasty of the Kingdom of Pergamon, and Macedon.	
Feet partly of iron and partly of baked clay: Divided Kingdoms	A little horn came out among the **ten**. Three of the first were uprooted.	A little horn came out among the **ten** and are given power to lead. Three of the first (four) were uprooted but from the tenth, seven will be led by the little horn.	Current and future Peace Treaties that are formed
GOD's Kingdom: Daniel 2:44-45	The Everlasting Kingdom of GOD	The Prince of Peace Second Coming and the establish-ment of HIS Kingdom.	Future

There are other related scriptures, but I only took the three
to conclude why I saw myself in Turkey. Daniel 7:24 says,

"The ten horns are ten kings
Who shall arise from this kingdom.
And another shall rise after them;
He shall be different from the first ones,
And shall subdue three kings."

Remember, Alexander the Great did conquer the Turkish, and upon his
death four kingdoms were formed, but they were conquered by Ancient
Rome. Ten horns will come from this kingdom of Rome (a new rising
world power) which already has the four Grecian Empire Kingdoms in it
(Turkey is included). When it comes to the book of Daniel, Daniel says
from these ten kingdoms another shall rise after them (the 11th) who shall
be from among the first but different from them (still the 10th). He shall
subdue his first three, and seven will be left. He will be crowned and lead
the remaining. On the other hand based Genesis 25:25 which narrates
Esau's birth, "Now the first came forth red, all over like a hairy garment;
and they named him Esau." ... The name Edom is also attributed to Esau,
meaning "red" (Heb: `admoni); the same color used to describe the color of
the hairs of Esau. The Edomite groups were present in Ancient Times and
their geographical area today is what is now known as Turkey.

Going back to the Turkish link to Daniel 7:7-8, the conclusion is that
although Alexander the Great was not himself Turkish, he was Greek and
considered himself Greek (as all Macedonian kings did), his Empire did
come to include what is now known as Turkey. This means Turkey will

play a very significant role in the prophecy of Daniel 7:7-8. The Euphrates river where i saw myself in the dream is the river that also flows generally southward through southeastern Turkey around Sanliurfa.

Geographical Location and Genealogy of Turkey and Esau:

"Turkey encompasses a land bridge that connects Europe with the Middle East, and its inhabitants have always been torn between identifying with its eastern Muslim neighbors and western trading partners. This Turkic empire grew to encompass North Africa east to the Euphrates River (Refer to Revelation 6:12 on apocalyptic events concerning this river and its drying up to prepare way for the kings of the east) and north into central Europe.

"When it comes to the genealogy of its origin, I encourage you to read Genesis 36 which gives the genealogy of Esau, the son of Isaac and brother of Jacob. This genealogy, in a book primarily concerned with Israel, was recorded because the children of Esau were a prominent people at the time and would continue to play an important role in Israel's future. Esau was also named Edom (Genesis 25:30). When it comes to his wishes for his brother, Jacob, read Genesis 27:41 so you can understand future prophecies. When Genesis 36 was recorded, the bulk of the Edomites lived at Mt. Seir, southeast of Palestine. There, the kingdom of Edom was established. But the Edomites did not stay there."

This prophecy is recorded in Genesis 27:39-41. There are more prophecies concerning Edom, and specifically Teman, in Obadiah. In verses 11 and

13, the Bible prophesies that the descendants of Edom would control an important "gate" and "crossway." Another prophecy in Psalm 83 indicates that Edom would also be near Moab and the Ammonites, which is modern-day Jordan, and also close to the Ishmaelites, modern-day Saudi Arabia. The only country that can fulfill these prophecies, and therefore be the descendants of Edom, is Turkey

When we read about the relationship between the Turks and the Ottomans, we read that the Ottoman Empire was founded in Anatolia, the location of modern-day Turkey. Thus, a new empire was born from within Anatolia: The Ottoman Empire. This was the Turkic empire that grew to encompass North Africa east to the Euphrates River and north into central Europe. During their rise, the Ottomans obtained the title of caliph, the spiritual head of all Islam. The empire lasted for 600 years, until the Allied powers dissolved it at the end of World War I. At the start of World War I, the Ottoman Empire was already in decline. The Ottoman Empire officially ended in 1922 when the title of Ottoman was eliminated.

Going back to the Promised Land of Israel, over the years from the times of King Solomon, the land was ruled by different kings. During the times of JESUS, the king was King Herod Antipas who was the son of Herod the Great and his Roman army – this King was not in the genealogical line of David.

After Jesus died, and HIS resurrection, going back to HIS FATHER in Heaven, the dispersion of the nation of Israel began with the purpose of spreading the Gospel to all nations. In the 7th century, the land was taken over by the Muslims. Later, the land would change hands a few times until the Ottoman Empire took control in 1517. The Ottoman Empire ruled until 1917.

The children of Israel, through sin, were driven out of the Promised Land that belonged with their birthright. The Turks came to power and dominion and for many centuries possessed that land. Those descendants, the Turkish people, occupied Palestine 400 years before Britain took it. Esau's descendants have always lusted for that land, the central promise of the birthright!

Turkey was declared a republic on October 29, 1923, when Mustafa Kemal Atatürk, an army officer, founded the independent Republic of Turkey. For the last century, his successors have built Turkey into a strong regional power, a counterbalance in the Middle East to Iran and Saudi Arabia. During the times of the book of Acts, Turkey was known as Antioch (Refer to Acts 11:26).

The reason I have diverted slightly to draw attention to the history of Turkey is because Turkey will play a key part as a major controlled gateway to access the promised land to fulfill the 70th week of Daniel 9:27 in the End Time Prophecies since in the past they ruled the biblical Promised Land for 400 years after Israel's dispersion due to their sin against GOD.

Note that the above indicate Isaac's dying prophecy, where he foretold that Esau's descendants would come to a time when they should have dominion, and then break the yoke of the Israelites off their necks. That has happened. Jacob (Israel) and Esau (the Edomites) are the first set of twins mentioned in the Bible. In Genesis 25, their mother (Rebekah) is told that she has two nations in her womb.

Apart from Daniel 7:7-8, the prophecy of Daniel 8, of the Ram and Goat, has come to pass according to Daniel 8:20-21.

In Conclusion: GOD has revealed that the Ram and the He-Goat Kingdoms has already passed by there is a linked to the latter 10 Kingdoms of the End Times and the answer is found in Psalm 83:6-8. The Ten Nations mentioned there are nations confederacy prophesied by the Psalmist to wage war against Israel. The nations mentioned below did not form any alliance in the past according to biblical readings, these nations still need to form the prophesized alliance of Ten Nations during the Great Tribulations. These are :-

1. The Tabernacles of Edom (now the located at Turkey near Euphrates River where the battle of Armageddon will take place and many people will be killed in this River as Turkey will be a gateway). We already know that the Edomites comes from Esau as indicated in Genesis 36:1.

2. The Ishmaelite's who came from Ismael (refer to Genesis 25:12-18), this includes other couple of neighboring nations like Saudi Arabia.

3. The Moabites who came from Lot's son by his eldest daughter (refer to Genesis 19:37), nations around Jordan.

4. Hagarenes the descendants of Hagar, being the branch of Ismael (Genesis 17:20), the Syria Nation.

5. Gebal where the land of the Gebalites, and all Lebanon, toward the sunrise, from Baal Gad below Mount Hermon as far as the entrance to Hamath are indicated in Joshua 13:5.

6. Ammonites who came from Lot by his younger daughter (refer to Genesis 19:38), nations around Jordan.

7. Amelekites who came from Esau (Refer to Genesis 36:12), this is also related to Turkey as indicated under Edom.

8. Philistines who are the descendants of Ham (Refer to Genesis 10:14) and this is Gaza.

9. Tyre who used to occupy the land beyond the Northern Boarder of Israel (Refer to Joshua 19:29; Ezekiel 27-28) and today we see this land as Southern Lebanon.

10. Asshur who came from Shem (Refer to Genesis 10:22), I was reading that during the first world war Germany turned to Soviet Russia or USSR with an offer of cooperation. The restoration of the past is seen under Assher.

In Genesis 27:40 we read the following:- 41 So Esau hated Jacob because of the blessing with which his father blessed him, and Esau said in his heart, "The days of mourning for my father are at hand; then I will kill my brother Jacob."

DREAM #9:
THE VALLEY OF DRY BONES AND THE 144,000 SEALED

I would like to encourage you to read the whole of Ezekiel 36 and 37 because it talks about the message of hope (restoration) for Israel as a whole nation. This message was delivered by Ezekiel, talking about future restoration and hope for the people as he gives a vivid picture of our unchangeable faithfulness and the holiness of our Almighty GOD.

In both chapters, Ezekiel consoles the people by telling them that the day will come when GOD will restore Israel and Judah for HIS name's sake because HE chose Israel and Judah as one Holy Nation for HIMSELF. Anything that GOD said will come to pass as written in the scriptures. They will become GOD's people once again (refer to Isaiah 51:11), and GOD will be their King and their Shepherd. He will give HIS people a new heart to worship HIM, and HE will establish a New Kingdom under HIS rule.

During my research, as I was reading biblical commentators in line with what the Bible says, I found it is indicated that the Bible likens the nation of Israel to a fig tree as Jesus said in the book of Matthew. A fig tree produces both good and bad (inedible) fruit. So it was with the nation of Israel. Jews who were whole-hearted followers of GOD were likened to 'good figs', and rebellious Jews were likened to 'bad figs'. The Bible also says that at the end of this age, Israel will 'blossom and bud' and 'put forth new leaves' like a fig tree, and that this will be a sign of the imminent return of Israel's true Messiah – YESHUA (JESUS CHRIST). To put it simply, the Bible says that the End-Times events of the world will be intricately linked to modern Israel.

I t

was on the night of the 25th of December, 2012, where in my dream I was in a non-passenger rail train as a passenger. This train was moving, and it had to stop in each train station although there was no one in the train except me. What caught my attention is that all along the way, we passed a very plain field where there were no people living, the area seemed desert-like until after some time this train stopped in another station. At this station, I stepped out and the train left me there alone. I then walked in the direction of the appearing sun which I thought in the dream was east.

Not far from the station (about 100m from the train platform), I saw a valley, and as I come near it, I saw it was filled with old, dry human bones as if a long time ago there had been a war and people were killed and their bodies left there in that valley. No one was there as I entered the valley, but immediately after I entered, a Man wearing a long white robe similar to the robes that the Jewish people used to wear, appeared in the valley. HIS feet did not touch the ground – they were about a foot off the ground.

As I was still watching this Man, another scene came upon me, and I saw a movement in the bones where pieces of these human bones came together and formed a whole human skeleton whilst still lying on the ground. Then, skeletons as they were, they stood up, facing this Man who did not say a word to me though he was also facing east as I was. I then saw these skeletons in two groups, one in front (Judah) and the other at the back (Israel) (Refer to Zechariah 12:7). The ones who were closer to this Man gained flesh and the others followed; they became human beings. I then saw these people wearing normal clothes and they started to breathe as human beings and from then, they were able to move their heads to show that they were alive unlike before. They were all looking at this Man, extremely focused, and I was just there watching what was happening.

Immediately after that, they began to sing a worship song still looking at this Man, and the Man stood in front as if HE were a choir conductor, but this Man remained quiet. HE was not leading or conducting a choir, but these people were the ones who were singing voluntarily and in obedience to this Man. The Man did not say anything to me either, my purpose was just to witness what was happening. HIS feet did not touch the ground.

As I was listening to the singing, a noise from outside our house woke me up and that was the end of this dream. When I woke up, I tried to recall the song that was sang by these men, but without any success.

Everything written in this book is like a small direction arrow pointing the reader to the Holy Bible (the word of GOD). When you read the word of GOD, the HOLY SPIRIT is the ONE who will give you more revelation. Hence, I would really encourage you to read the whole of Ezekiel 36 and 37 as it talks about GOD's restoration of Israel as a nation. GOD wants HIS word to be sown in our spirit, so it is important for us to read HIS Word.

GOD said through the prophet in Zechariah 13:1 that,

> *"In that day a fountain shall be opened for the house of David and for the inhabitants of Jerusalem, for sin and for uncleanness."*

In the book of Ezekiel, Israel says they are cut-off, but GOD will pour out a fountain of cleansing power. This fountain symbolizes GOD's forgiveness by pouring His endless living water that would satisfy the thirsty completely as they drink from this fountain. Based on the dream and the reference to Ezekiel 37, "the valley of dry bones", this drinking from the fountain and conversion will happen very quickly after Israel is a whole nation in the latter days.

The certainty of this restoration encourages us in times of trials, hence this chapter is about GOD's restoration in the valley. Our Almighty GOD can see and hear the voice of a sparrow in the valley because GOD who created the mountains is still GOD in the valley no matter how deep or dark the valley may be. Below are only two examples of restorations that happened in the valley on individual persons and on a group of GOD's people.

DREAM #10: SEEING FOUR FACES OF CHRIST

One day, I had a dream in which I was living in a very densely populated township of South Africa. As I was outside the house that I lived in, I saw people who were busy with different activities like partying, watching weddings, children playing, and so forth.

As I was standing outside my little house, I saw four large, very visible human faces up in the sky which were placed in the four directions of the earth (north, south, east, and west). I then understood in the dream that these faces were the faces of the LORD JESUS which made me shout, telling others who were around me what I had seen as I was filled with joy. But people did not even bother to look or listen to what I was telling and showing them. In Matthew 24:37-40, JESUS said,

37"But as the days of Noah were, so also will the coming of the Son of Man be. 38For as in the days before the flood, they were eating and drinking, marrying and giving in marriage, until the day that Noah entered the ark, 39and did not know until the flood came and took them all away, so also will the coming of the Son of Man be. 40Then two men will be in the field: one will be taken (raptured) and the other left."

DREAM #11:
SEEING BELIEVERS
CAUGHT-UP OR RAPTURED

Rapture means to be taken from one place to another. In April 2010, I had another dream where I saw people being caught-up or raptured into the air (they were taken very quickly). This happened during the day where again we were busy with our daily activities. When this happened, again I was outside the house and suddenly I saw people being caught up or pulled into the sky very quickly, separated from others who were left on the earth. It came to my mind in the dream that the pulling power was the power of the HOLY SPIRIT HIMSELF.

This pulling power was a visible snatching-up (like a fast wind) and these people were pulled up to the sky in the twinkling of an eye as it happened. The last person I saw being taken, just next to where I stood, was a woman in her mid-sixties holding a baby. I understood in the dream that the baby was not hers, but the baby was her grandchild, though the mother of the baby was not there. This woman was caught up together with the baby in her arms in front of our eyes. I saw a picture of this rapture exactly like the one below.

As I was still watching, I noticed that others were not taken, and I was one of them. Because I knew about the rapture as a Christian, I became worried that I was not caught up. I looked up into the sky, filled with these worries, thinking what am I going to do? Discouragement came into my mind and strength left me, and I was powerless.

Right there, the small voice of the HOLY SPIRIT assured me that I am only witnessing what is going to happen so that I can tell others, HE assured me that I will be caught up when the time comes. That encouragement immediately gave me strength and boldness again in the dream. Another woman who was standing next to me was a tavern owner and she was left as well. This woman was so shocked, and I explained to her what was happening because at that moment I had strength. I told her that she was left because she had not received Jesus as her Lord and Savior, and the woman was helpless.

I woke up and immediately went to my sister who is a Pastor of a Pentecostal Church (Pastor Emily Dhlamini) I had attended since birth. I explained the dream to her, and we prayed together. Because I did not want to take any responsibility for this woman's salvation (the tavern owner), after prayer, I immediately went to the woman who was not caught up. She was with her lover, and I began to witness to both of them about Christ and salvation. Sadly, she passed on few years after I witnessed to her.

I may not worry so much about the dreams as I said earlier that anything written in this book is like a small direction arrow pointing to the Word of GOD. The whole thing makes me focus on reading the Holy Bible and understanding exactly what is said in the Word. That is where 1 Thessalonians 4:16-17 comes in. Sometimes GOD gives us dreams and visions so we can start to think about the real situation as it is written in His Holy Word.

The Thessalonians were wondering why many of their fellow believers had died and what would happen to them when CHRIST returned. Paul explained, as written in the abovementioned scripture, that Christians must not worry about death because there is a great hope of the resurrection of the dead when CHRIST comes. The Bible says that those who are still living when the LORD returns will not meet HIM ahead of those who have died. The LORD HIMSELF will come down from heaven with a commanding shout, where the dead in CHRIST will rise first from their graves, then, together with them, those who are still alive will be caught up in the clouds to meet the LORD in the air and to be with HIM forever.

This precious, wonderful dream-vision captured my mind because it gave me an exciting hope about the rapture. It is important for us to know that JESUS does not force anyone to follow HIM, it is our choice whether we follow HIM or not. If we choose to follow HIM, we will be saved and receive eternal life, peace, and joy in HIM.

Our ALMIGHTY GOD is the creator of the universe. The Bible begins with the majestic story of the creation of the universe, and it concludes with HIM creating a new heaven and a new earth, for the past was filled with sin. This is tremendous hope and encouragement for those who are saved in CHRIST through the HOLY SPIRIT because JESUS assures us in John 18:36 that HIS kingdom is not of this world. When we are with GOD, with our sins forgiven and our future secured, we will be made perfect like CHRIST, enjoying the eternal life in HIS kingdom which has already begun in the hearts of believers. The only entrance requirements to this magnificent place are repentance and the rebirth.

We can only live victoriously when we acknowledge the presence of the HOLY SPIRIT in us who will help us to overcome evil forces, provided we allow HIM – our main responsibilities are to allow HIM and surrender all to HIM – to lead us. And we always need to pray for courage to do what is right no matter what pressure we are faced with.

The Bible tells us that it is in this dispensation where we need to know that those who endure to the end and remain faithful will be rewarded by GOD. JESUS says in Revelation 3:20-22,

"20Behold, I stand at the door and knock. If anyone hears My voice and opens the door, I will come into him and dine with him, and he with Me. 21To him who overcomes I will grant to sit with Me on My throne, as I also overcame and sat down with My Father on His throne. 22He, who has an ear, let him hear what the Spirit says to the churches."

In closing, it seems evident that all prophecies are fulfilled leading to the rapture of the saints. We read in 1 Thessalonians 4:13-18 that the Coming of the LORD is at hand and all those who believe in CHRIST – meaning all the dead from the time of creation, and all the living – will be caught up together into the clouds to meet the LORD in the air where our bodies will be changed from perishable to imperishable (1 Corinthians 15:50-58).

Romans 8:22-24 supports the above Rapture Scriptures as it says,

"22For we know that the whole creation groans and labours with birth pangs together until now. 23Not only that, but we also who have the first fruits of the Spirit, even we ourselves groan within ourselves, eagerly waiting for the adoption, the redemption of our body. 24For we were saved in this hope, but hope that is seen is not hope; for why one still hopes for what he sees?"

Other interpretations further explain that not only the corrupt, depraved creations, but we who are redeemed, also suffer and wait for final redemption of the body (1 Corinthians 15:50-58; Philippians 3:21).

If you would like to read more, you can refer to the book that I was led by the HOLY SPIRIT to write in 2014, titled "The Work of the HOLY SPIRIT Today: About Salvation and the Baptism of the HOLY SPIRIT.

DREAM #12: THE PROMISED HEAVENLY HOMES

Whilst I was working in New Zealand, one day I had a dream related to John 14:1-4 when JESUS was comforting HIS believers and said:-

"Do not let your hearts be troubled. You believe in God[a]; believe also in me. 2 My Father's house has many rooms; if that were not so, would I have told you that I am going there to prepare a place for you? 3 And if I go and prepare a place for you, I will come back and take you to be with me that you also may be where I am. 4 You know the way to the place where I am going."

In the dream I saw myself in the third heaven and we were in a bus. We were not many in this luxurious touring bus as we were about seven. I would say it is obvious that the bus tour driver could be an angel. I saw the streets in heaven were pure gold with beautiful grass on the sides of the street pure green. There were extremely beautiful houses or mansions but there were not the same. Most were empty but in few of them there were occupants. Our bus was not allowed to touch the golden streets, it was moving without touching the street, We wanted to go out and view the mansions, but we were told it is not yet the appointed time, we were not allowed to go out of the bus. Right there I saw a deceased school friend of mine whose name was Grace, but I was not allowed to talk to her The but took us on tour until I woke up.

The primary purpose of writing this entire book is to indicate to those who have not received salvation that today is the right time to receive it as it is still available. In the book of Amos 8:12, the prophet highlights that the days are coming, declared the LORD, when men will stagger from sea to sea and wander from North to East searching for the Word of the LORD. But they will not find it. Those who have received the Word with gladness are the ones who will be Raptured. Believers are aware that the Rapture will happen anytime, and it is only GOD who knows the timing. If one is not Raptured, Revelation 6 and 7 shows that the grace of GOD will still be there since the HOLY SPIRIT will still be ministering to individual's hearts and to nations (in the absence of the Raptured Saints) for salvation, although they will receive as martyr or being killed for the religious belief. GOD does love us including our beloved brothers and sisters that we are praying for everyday who are not yet saved, though they will see the unfolding of the tribulation events after Rapture (which includes the martyr events described under Revelation 6 – 19). In Revelation 14:5 we see the last Rapture of the 144 000 to the Heavenly City of Jerusalem for a short while before the Second Coming of CHRIST (Hebrews 12:22) who are the Remnant of Judah.

In closing, it seems evident that all prophecies are fulfilled leading to the rapture of the saints. We read in 1 Thessalonians 4:13-18 that the Coming of the Lord is at hand and all those who believe in CHRIST – meaning all the dead from the time of creation and all the living – will be caught up together into the clouds to meet the Lord in the air where our bodies will be changed from perishable to imperishable (1 Corinthians 15:50-58).

In Hebrews 12:22; Romans 11:26; Revelation 1:14 Saints (the chosen priests and kings as it is written in Revelation 1:6) will be in the Mount Sion after Rapture which is the Heavenly City of Jerusalem (the Earthly one being a copy of the Heavenly one), the City of the Living GOD. In the City there are innumerable angles and the general assembly and the church of the first born children of the Most HIGH GOD (Colossians 1:18) since the LORD HIMSELF has preeminence in all things as the HEAD of the church. This is where the spirits of just men will be made perfect as written in Revelation 6:9-11 and Hebrews 12:23, these are the ones whose names are written in the Book of the LAMB, the Book of life (Luke 10:20 and Revelation 20:15).

This does not end there, in Jude 14 where the verse mentions the prophecy of Enoch, the 7th from Adam, who said, "Behold, the LORD comes with ten thousands of HIS Saints" indicating the Second Coming together with Saints of Revelation 1:6 (the kings and priests). HE has already made us to be kings and priests in HIS Kingdom, we are being equipped to work with HIM now and in after HIS Second Coming here on earth in the City of Jerusalem where JESUS the Son of David will rule the whole world from the City as it is written in Zachariah 8:3:-

3 "Thus says the Lord:

'I will return to Zion, And dwell in the midst of Jerusalem.
Jerusalem shall be called the City of Truth, The Mountain
of the Lord of hosts, The Holy Mountain.'

The dream below explains that in the New Jerusalem that will come down from Heaven to earth, there will be no need for sun or moon because the glory of GOD will be its light, and the LAMB JESUS will be its lamp. The radiance and life will come from GOD HIMSELF.

DREAM #13: THE NEW JERUSALEM

As we are waiting and hoping for this rapture, we are encouraged in Revelation 19:7-8,

> *"⁷Let us be glad and rejoice and give Him glory, for the marriage of the Lamb has come, and His wife has made herself ready."*
> *⁸And to her it was granted to be arrayed in fine linen, clean and bright, for the fine linen is the righteous acts of the saints."*

In my dream of October, 2012, we were living normally, as we are today. I was living near the sea and just next to the sea was an excessively big boat made up of wood, but not fully watertight, as I could see some gaps between the timber. Amazingly, inside this boat, there was water, and I realized that this water was not leaking in spite of the gaps between the wood. It came to my mind that it must be GOD who was holding this water in the boat. As I explored the boat with some others, we were told that everyone must run into a big church building nearby for safety because the water in the boat will be released. Many were far away, and did not hear the message, but we ran into the church building. When we entered the church, the door of the church was closed behind us. The water of the boat was then released and flooded the whole earth. All people who were not inside the church died whilst we watched from the church windows – though the height of this water outside was well above the church windows. We had to wait for days until the water dried up.

After some days, we went outside and began a new life again, and the population grew. During that time, I was not living near the sea, but I was living near the same church building which this time was situated in the Middle East. In the dream, I knew it was situated near the center of the earth. I was aware that the LORD JESUS was there as well, though I couldn't see HIM literally. HE was in authority over the whole earth, not just the Middle East. As people were busy doing their day-to-day things, we were told that we needed to run to the church again for safety, which we did. Many of us were thinking about our relatives who were far away and who did not hear the message so they could be saved as well, but it was too late. We then entered this church building which had an open hall without any dividing walls. Our purpose was to do nothing, except to be saved. After the door was closed, fire came from heaven and I really sensed a pull from my spirit that the LORD was there and in authority to destroy all evil, keeping us safe in the church. This fire covered the whole earth and consumed all living things and elements that were on the earth as we watched again from the church and were not affected by this fire at all.

After some days, quietness came and there was no fire anymore. This time, we did not go out of the church as we had after the floods but the church developed walls inside and it became like a city where we all began to establish our lives. The church roof disappeared and a new environment was felt with freedom, security, and quietness in a brotherly-spirit environment. I saw the sun coming through from the sky into this new city before I woke up.

Matthew 3 opens with words spoken by the voice of the one who was crying in the wilderness, John the Baptist, preparing the way of the LORD JESUS and making HIS paths straight. John preached a central message to multitudes saying,

"Repent: for the kingdom of heaven is at hand."

Again, in Matthew 4:17, we read that JESUS, being full of the HOLY GHOST, began HIS ministry with a powerful preaching of this central message saying,

"Repent: for the kingdom of heaven is at hand."

As I related in one of my dreams, the LORD JESUS appeared in human form, preaching the Good News of the Kingdom, saying,

"Repent: for the kingdom of heaven is at hand."

It is also written in Luke 4:43 that when JESUS began HIS ministry, the crowd in Galilee tried to keep HIM from leaving them and HE said to them,

"I must preach the Kingdom of GOD to the other cities also, because for this purpose I have been sent."

As I close this Devine Dreams book, in accordance to the book of Numbers 6:24-27

To the reader of this book:-

May the LORD bless you and keep you,

May the LORD make HIS Face shine upon
you, and may HE be gracious to you,

May the LORD lift up HIS countenance upon you and give you peace.

I say all of this in JESUS NAME. Amen

JESUS PRAYED FOR ONE BODY

Jesus prayed in John 17:20-21 and said,

"I do not pray for these (the disciples) alone, but also for those who will believe in Me through their word; that they all may be one, as You, Father, are in Me, and I in You; that they also may be one in Us, that the world may believe that You sent Me."

Jesus as the Son of God, He was sent by God to the earth. From His teachings during His ministry here on earth, His greatest desire for His disciples was that they would become one because the Father, Son and the Holy Spirit are united in harmony and in love and this tells us that they are the strongest of all unions. He also wants us to unify against division to demonstrate a powerful witness of the reality of God's love in us.

As the scripture says, He did not only pray for disciples, but He also prayed for all who believed in Him even today. Remember in John 16:9 we are told that the world's sin is to refuse to believe that Jesus is the

Son of God and that He was sent by God to die for our sins, whom God raised physically from the dead through His Spirit (also see Romans 10:9). There is no doubt to us as His followers that He is the Son of God since we do believe that Jesus was sent by God. Christianity is all about believing through faith any word that proceeds from the Holy Bible as the Word of God, and His Word is truth. Through this believing, He prayed for unity among today's believers, and based on the believers' unity, the believers will abide in Christ through His Spirit because we cannot bear any fruit without this abiding and there won't be any unity without this abiding. It is through faith that we can abide in Him so He can lead us to a personal and a dynamic relationship to the Father because we believe that He is from God the Father. We can only know unity among ourselves if we are living in union with God since each branch living in union with the vine is united with all other branches of the same kind and producing the same fruit.

Ephesians 4:2-6 says,

"…with all lowliness and gentleness, with longsuffering; bearing with one another in love, endeavoring to keep the unity of the Spirit in the bond of peace. There is one body and one Spirit, just as you were called in one hope of your calling; one Lord, one faith, one baptism; one God and Father of all, who is above all, and through all, and in you all."

One of the Holy Spirit important roles is to reconcile us back to God and to build unity among the believers. He leads, but we have to be willing to be led and to do our part through building of this unity and peace among us. We can only do that by focusing on God not on our selfish deeds because we are all united under one body. It is done because Jesus has already prayed about it, ours is just to preserve and act on what He has already said and did.

In John 17:4, Jesus is praying for Himself telling the Father that He brought glory to Him by completing the work that the Father gave Him. We were unified through the work of the cross that was completed when Jesus said 'it is finished' and the Father answered His prayer. This also shows Jesus Divinity, any word that He has spoken will not return to Him void because He is the Son of God, when He prayed, the Father answered already, hence we don't need to struggle for unity but to thank Him for what He has already done, and act according to His words knowing that the Holy Spirit is here to help us (John 16:7). We see this Divine assurance in John 11:41-42 when Jesus prayed He lifted up His eyes and said,

"Father, I thank You that You have heard Me. And I know that You always hear Me, but because of the people who are standing by I said this, that they may believe that You sent Me."

This shows a perfect harmony and unity between the Father, the Son through the Holy Spirit that we need to follow because Jesus knew that anything He did was according to the Will of His Father and His Father always answered His prayer (Mark 11:24). We see a unity that could not be broken between them. He has already prayed for unity among us, which we need to embrace and honour His prayer. We need to allow the Holy Spirit to work through us in unifying the Body of Christ under one Head and One Spirit.

WALLS OF DENOMINATIONS

It is so interesting when you read about the work of the Holy Spirit even in the Old Testament to backup what Paul says in Ephesians 4 that,

" there is one body and one Spirit, just as you were called in one hope of your calling; one Lord, one faith, one baptism; one God and Father of all, who is above all, and through all, and in you all".

In the Old Testament we read in Numbers 11:17 during the tough times when the mixed multitude complained for the provision of meat that God instructed Moses to gather seventy elders who will help him not to bear the burdens alone. Note what God said to Moses in verse 17,

"Then I will come down and talk with you there. I will take of the Spirit that is upon you and will put the same upon them; and they shall bear the burden of the people with you, that you may not bear it yourself alone."

That was a promise to Moses and this promise was fulfilled in verse 25 as the scripture says,

"Then the Lord came down in the cloud, and spoke to him, and took of the Spirit that was upon him, and placed the same upon the seventy elders; and it happened, when the Spirit rested upon them, that they prophesied, although they never did so again."

These scriptures shows that, God want us to be filled with One Spirit so we could be unified into one body and again it shows that we can only operate in harmony under the same Spirit. In other words, it is not easy to unify or even understand one another if we are not operating under the same Spirit, should this be the case, conflicts will always arise since we all know that unity is power.

1 Corinthians 12:14 says,

"For by one Spirit we were all baptized into one body - whether Jews or Greeks, whether slaves or free - and have all been made to drink into one Spirit. Now the body is not made up of one part but many".

The body of Christ, which is the church is composed of many types of people from a variety of backgrounds with a multitude of different gifts and abilities. It is easy for these differences to divide people, as was the case in the Corinthian church. Despite the differences, all believers have one thing in common - faith in Christ. On this essential truth, the church finds unity. The scripture above shows that all believers are baptized under one Spirit into one body. In the church, we don't lose our individual identities, but we have an overriding oneness in Christ. When we become Christians, He took up residence in us, and we were born into God's family - meaning that, each of us has received the same Holy Spirit. As members of God's family, we may have different interests and gifts, but we are united by the Spirit into one body which also breaks the walls of denominations among all who are Christ followers.

In conclusion, Jesus thought that, the first commandment is to love God followed by the second one, which is to love our neighbors. In other words, the love from God is perfect, once the Spirit of Christ dwells in us, then we will be able to share His love to others because without Him it will be impossible. Before Jesus appointed His disciples, they were not in unity until Jesus unified them in spite of their differences. Remember some did not like Matthew because he was a despised tax collector, hated by many due to the type of work he was involved in, but after Jesus appointed His disciples, they were unified.

This shows us that without God, there won't be unity among us but because the Holy Spirit is in us, there is one body under one Spirit and the unity that the Holy Spirit is creating also breaks the walls of denominations among believers as we are all united under one Head. The walls of denominations are weakening the Body of Christ because believers begin to focus on the walls rather than embracing the fact that Christ has already prayed for these walls to be broken so that one Body is sustained under one Spirit. The walls of denominations were broken down by Christ on the cross and the Holy Spirit is uniting the Church under one Spirit. Based on the scriptures, it shows that Jesus is coming for one Church body under one Spirit not multiple bodies of Christ. We are all under one body under one Head which is Christ.

JESUS is Coming back for ONE Body not for many small bodies or many divided parts of the body. HE Commanded the Body to be one under ONE HEAD and ONE SPIRIT.

ACKNOWLEDGMENTS:

I want to thank GOD the HOLY SPIRIT for HIS fulfilment of Joel 2:28 in my life. HIS Word is truth and it will come to pass as it is. To receive Devine Dreams is for all flesh since the Out Pouring is happening right now to the whole world as long as we play our parts by opening our hearts to receive. Without the HOLY SPIRIT I know nothing and can do nothing. The writers in the bible received Devine Revelation from the HOLY SPIRIT in their writings and this is still happening even today since we were appointed for this End Time hour under HIS Devine Grace.